Events of 1920

News for every day of the year

The Unknown Warrior lies in state, Westminster Abbey, London, 11 November 1920.

Events of 1920

News for every day of the year

His Majesty
the King-Emperor
George V
of Great Britain and Ireland.

By Hugh Morrison

MONTPELIER PUBLISHING

Front cover (clockwise from left): Poster for 1920 Olympics. Tomb of the Unknown Warrior, Westminster Abbey. Film star Mary Pickford. Programme for the the 1920 Baseball World Series showing Babe Ruth.

Back cover (clockwise from top): Poster for *The Mark of Zorro*. *Forward, Warsaw!* by Zdzisław Jasiński. US tennis champ Bill Tilden. US President Warren G Harding. A 'Black and Tan' (Royal Irish Constabulary Special Reserve officer), Dublin. *Burial of the Unknown Warrior* by Frank G Salisbury.

Image credits: (in order of appearance) Front cover: Zombikombi 1959. Interior: Horace Nicholls, Agence de Presse Meurisse. C Thomas. Syrio, George Grantham Bane, Pierre Choumoff, Lothar Shaak, Allan Warren, Brown Brothers, John Warwick Brooke/Imperial War Museum, Wizardman, Herbert Lambert/National Portrait Gallery, George Grantham Bain, Jac. de Nijs / Anefo, Scottish National Gallery.

Published in Great Britain by Montpelier Publishing.

Printed and distributed by Amazon KDP.

This edition © 2019. All rights reserved.

ISBN: 9781696025119

January 1920

Thursday 1: The Soviet army increases its divisions on the Polish front from 4 to 20 as the Polish-Soviet war intensifies.

Friday 2: 4,025 suspected communists are arrested across the USA in what is known as the 'first red scare'.

Science fiction writer Isaac Asimov, inventor of the Laws of Robotics, is born Petrovichi, Russia (died 1992).

A *Chicago Tribune* cartoon of the Red Scare era, showing an immigrant with a bomb instead of a head entering the USA.

Saturday 3: Polish mathematician Zygmunt Janiszewski, originator of Janiszewski's Theorem, dies of influenza aged 31.

Sunday 4: 700 people die in a 6.4 magnitude earthquake near Jalapa, Mexico.

Polish volunteer troops, including a rare woman soldier (second from left).

January 1920

Monday 5: Film drama *A Daughter of Two Worlds* starring Norma Talmadge and Jack Crosby is released in the USA.

Tuesday 6: Spiritualist medium Doris Stokes is born in Grantham, Lincolnshire, England (died 1987).

Wednesday 7: Sir Lionel Pilkington, inventor of the float-glass manufacturing process, is born in Calcutta, India (died 1995).

Thursday 8: The last engagement of US forces in the Allied Intervention following the Russian Revolution, takes place at the Battle of Posolskeya.

Silent film star Norma Talmadge, one of the most popular screen actresses of the early 1920s.

Friday 9: George Polley, the 'Human Fly' climbs the Woolworth Building in New York City; he gets as far as the 30th floor before being arrested.

35 people are killed when the British cargo steamer *Treveal* sinks in the English Channel.

Actor Clive Dunn OBE, (Lance Corporal Jones in the BBC comedy series *Dad's Army*), is born in London (died 2012).

Saturday 10: The First World War officially ends as the 1919 Treaty of Versailles goes into effect.

Sunday 11: The Democratic Republic of Azerbaijan is formally recognised by European powers.

January 1920

Monday 12: James Farmer, American civil rights activist and co-campaigner with Martin Luther King Jr, is born in Marshall, Texas (died 1999).

Tuesday 13: *The New York Times* mocks inventor Robert H Goddard's recently published proposals for rocket propulsion. The paper does not issue a formal apology until 1969, when the Apollo 11 rocket lands on the moon.

Wednesday 14: John Francis Dodge, co-founder of the Dodge Brothers motor company, dies aged 55.

Thursday 15: The US Navy permits the wearing of sailor's caps showing ship's names, banned for security reasons in the First World War.

Jazz singer Thelma Carpenter is born in New York City (died 1997).

Actress Pamela Cundell (Mrs Fox in *Dad's Army*) is born in Croydon, Surrey (died 2015).

Friday 16: Prohibition begins in the USA, as the Eighteenth Amendment to the Constitution goes into effect at midnight.

Saturday 17: All home teams are undefeated in all of this day's 20 matches in the English Football league.

Mary Pickford (left) and Katherine Griffith in *Pollyanna*.

Sunday 18: Film drama *Pollyanna* is released in the USA, starring Mary Pickford in the title role.

January 1920

Monday 19: The United States Senate votes against joining the League of Nations (the forerunner of the United Nations).

Tuesday 20: Film director Federico Fellini (*La Dolce Vita*) is born in Rimini, Italy (died 1993).

Actor DeForest Kelley (Dr Leonard 'Bones' McCoy in *Star Trek*) is born in Toccoa, Georgia (died 1999).

Wednesday 21: The Paris Peace Conference, which produced the Treaty of Versailles ending the First World War, is brought to a close. The USA does not conclude its own peace treaty with Germany until 25 August 1921.

De Forrest Kelley.

Thursday 22: The National Party of Australia (formerly the Country Party) is founded with William McWilliams as leader.

Kaiser Wilhelm II: the Allied attempt to bring him to trial for war crimes is unsuccessful.

Friday 23: A request to extradite the Kaiser for trial by the Allies is refused by the government of the neutral Netherlands, where the German ruler has been living in exile since 1918.

Saturday 24: Italian modernist painter and sculptor Amedeo Modigliani dies aged 35.

Sunday 25: As the economic crisis worsens in Germany, employers are ordered by the government to dismiss all single women with two or fewer dependents and women whose husbands are in work.

January/February 1920

Monday 26: In a fit of depression, Jeanne Hébuterne, fiancee of artist Amedeo Modigliani, throws herself out of a fifth floor window after his funeral, killing herself and her unborn child.

Tuesday 27: The comedy drama film *Suds* starring Mary Pickford is released in the USA.

Wednesday 28: The Spanish Foreign Legion is formed.

Thursday 29: Cartoonist Walt Disney begins his first job, with the Kansas City Slide Company.

Friday 30: The Mazda car company is founded in Hiroshima, Japan.

Saturday 31: Footballer Bert 'The Cat' Williams MBE of Wolverhampton Wanderers is born in Staffordshire, England. At the time of his death in 2014 he was the oldest living England international.

Sunday 1: The South African Air Force is established, the second in the world after Britain's Royal Air Force.

Walt Disney's first business card, featuring a self portrait of the cartoonist.

February 1920

Monday 2: The Tartu Peace Treaty is signed, ending Estonia's war of independence from Russia.

Tuesday 3: British, French and US ships begin the evacuation of refugees fleeing communism from Odessa in the Crimea.

Wednesday 4: Two South African pilots, Lt Col Pierre Van Ryneveld and Lt Col Christopher Joseph Quintin Brand set out from London to Cape Town, South Africa, in a Vickers Vimy named the *Silver Queen.* The flight time is 109 hours but the actual trip takes 45 days due to two crash landings.

Brand and Van Ryneveld with the *Silver Queen.*

Thursday 5: British comedian and writer Frank Muir (*The Glums, Take It From Here*) is born in London (died 1998).

Friday 6: The Saarland region of Germany, on the French border, is occupied by British and French troops under the League of Nations governing mandate.

Saturday 7: Two senior White Russians (anti-Communists), Admiral Kolchak and Viktor Pepelyayev are executed in Irkutsk, Siberia.

Sunday 8: The Red Army captures Odessa; all White Russian forces (those loyal to the Czar) flee the Ukraine.

February 1920

Monday 9: The Svalbard Treaty recognises the sovereignty of Norway over Spitzbergen.

Tuesday 10: Polish troops perform a ceremony known as 'Poland's Wedding to the Sea' celebrating the restitution of Polish access to the Baltic Sea via the Polish Corridor.

Polish troops perform the 'wedding to the sea'.

Wednesday 11: The Council of the League of Nations meets in London for the first time.

Thursday 12: The Conference of London takes place, in which British, French and Italian leaders discuss the future of the vanquished Ottoman Empire.

Friday 13: The first black baseball league, the National Negro League, is formed in the USA.

Saturday 14: The US League of Women Voters is formed in Chicago.

Sunday 15: 30 members of the Irish Republican Army (IRA) attack a police station at Shantonagh, County Monaghan, wounding four officers and stealing their weaponry.

February 1920

Monday 16: Anna Mae Hays, the US army's first woman general, is born in Buffalo, New York.

Tuesday 17: A woman named Anna Anderson attempts suicide in Berlin; after being committed to an asylum she claims to be Grand Duchess Anastasia of Russia. After seven years of media attention, the claims are ruled false by a German court.

Wednesday 18: Actor Jack Pallance (*City Slickers*) is born in Pennsylvania (died 2006).

Thursday 19: The United States Senate refuses to ratify the Treaty of Versailles. A separate US-German peace treaty is not signed until 25 August 1921.

Friday 20: 114 people are killed in an earthquake in Gori, in the Republic of Georgia.

Saturday 21: Darius Milhaud and Jean Cocteau's ballet *Les Maries de la Tour Eiffel* premieres in Paris.

Sunday 22: The first artificial rabbit is used in a dog racing track, in Emeryville, California.

From top: General Anna Mae Hays. Jean Cocteau. Jack Pallance.

February 1920

Monday 23: All 10 crew of the trawler *Strathord* are killed when their vessel hits a German mine in the North Sea off England's Yorkshire coast.

Britain's War Secretary, Winston Churchill, announces that the country's conscript army will be replaced by a volunteer force.

Tuesday 24: The German Workers' Party changes its name to the Nazi Party and adopts the National Socialist Programme of its publicity chief, Adolf Hitler.

Wednesday 25: Romanian troops leave Hungary, which they have occupied since August 1919.

Romanian troops on patrol in Budapest. Romanian forces leave on 25 February after occupying Hungary during an attempted Bolshevik uprising.

Sun Myung Moon, leader of the Unification Church (the 'Moonies') is born in Chongju, Korea (died 2012).

Thursday 26: Actor Tony Randall (Felix Unger in the TV series *The Odd Couple*) is born in Tulsa, Oklahoma (died 2004).

Friday 27: PC John Walsh of the Dublin Police is shot dead in an attack by IRA gunmen.

Saturday 28: Maurice Ravel's piano suite *Le Tombeau de Couperin* is performed for the first time, in Paris.

Sunday 29: The newly formed Republic of Czechoslovakia (established 1918) adopts its first constitution.

March 1920

Admiral Horthy.

Monday 1: Following the renunciation of the Hungarian throne by King Charles IV in 1918, Admiral Miklós Horthy becomes Regent of Hungary. He becomes known as 'the admiral without a navy in a kingdom without a king'.

Tuesday 2: Silent film star Mary Pickford divorces actor Owen Moore after nine years of marriage.

Wednesday 3: Actor James Doohan, ('Scotty' in *Star Trek*), is born in Vancouver, Canada.

James Doohan.

Thursday 4: The National Council of Catholic Women (NCCW) is founded in the USA. Meanwhile in Russia, Lenin announces, in anticipation of International Women's Day on 8 March, that communism will replace the 'domestic slavery' of women with 'socially productive labour'.

Friday 5: The case of Evans *v* Gore is heard in the US Supreme Court, which rules (on 1 June) that judges are subject to income tax.

Saturday 6: James Bond film director Lewis Gilbert (*You Only Live Twice, The Spy Who Loved Me, Moonraker*) is born in London, England.

Sunday 7: Following the withdrawal of British and French troops, the former Ottoman Empire possession of Syria declares itself an independent state under King Faisal.

March 1920

Monday 8: Protests are raised in the British parliament over plans to introduce a tax for motor cars, with one MP arguing against the idea because 'a motor car is now a means of locomotion used for convenience or necessity, and not as an indication of wealth'.

Tuesday 9: Constable Thomas Ryan (39) is killed during an IRA bomb attack on Hugginstown Barracks, County Kilkenny.

Wednesday 10: The British Parliament approves a grant of £20,000 for the forthcoming tour of HRH The Prince of Wales of the USA, Australia and New Zealand.

Thursday 11: Constable Timothy Scully of the Royal Irish Constabulary is shot dead in an IRA attack.

Friday 12: French artist Marchel Duchamp publishes his famous parody of the Mona Lisa in *319 Magazine*. It consists solely of the original painting with the addition of a moustache.

Saturday 13: The Kapp Putsch in Germany briefly overthrows the post-war Weimar Republic government in Berlin.

Sunday 14: Hank Ketcham, creator of the US newspaper cartoon strip Dennis the Menace, is born in Seattle, Washington (died 2001).

Given the option of remaining in Germany or becoming part of Denmark, the citizens of the Schleswig border region vote to remain part of Germany.

Marcel Duchamp's parody of the Mona Lisa.

March 1920

Monday 15: At least 15 people are killed when British and Indian forces occupy Turkey's capital Constantinople (Istanbul), as nationalists protest over plans to partition the country.

Tuesday 16: HRH Prince Edward, Prince of Wales, departs from Portsmouth on his tour of the USA, Australia and New Zealand.

Wednesday 17: The Ruhr Uprising: members of the communist volunteer force the Ruhr Red Army clash with the forces of the Kapp Putsch in Dortmund, Germany.

The Edith Cavell Memorial, London.

HM Queen Alexandra unveils the statue of the martyred Nurse Edith Cavell in Trafalgar Square, London. Nurse Cavell was executed in 1915 for assisting wounded Allied soldiers to escape from German-occupied Belgium.

Thursday 18: 19 sailors perish when the French freighter *Cordier* sinks off the coast of Alderney, Channel Islands.

Friday 19: The US Congress rejects the Treaty of Versailles.

Saturday 20: Lt Col Pierre van Ryneveld and Lt Col Christopher Joseph Quintin Brand complete the first flight from London to South Africa, taking 45 days due to two crash landings.

Sunday 21: French 'new wave' film director Eric Rohmer (*The Aviator's Wife*) is born in Nancy, France (died 2010).

March 1920

Monday 22: Actor Werner Klemperer (Colonel Klink in *Hogan's Heroes*) is born in Cologne, Germany (died 2000).

Tuesday 23: British comedy writer and actor Jimmy Edwards DFC (*Take it from Here, Whack-O!*) is born in Barnes, Surrey. (died 1988).

Wednesday 24: The first US coastguard air station is established at Morehead City, North Carolina.

Werner Klemperer.

Thursday 25: Hardline British auxiliary police officers arrive in Ireland to support the beleaguered Royal Irish Constabulary against IRA attacks; they are nicknamed the 'Black and Tans' because of the colour of their uniforms.

Friday 26: Jack Anthony wins the 79th Grand National horse race on Troytown.

Former Royal Irish Constabulary inspector and magistrate Alan Bell is ordered off a tram in Dublin and shot dead in the street by nationalist gunmen.

Jimmy Edwards.

Saturday 27: Following the collapse of the Kapp Putsch in Germany, moderate leftist social reformer Hermann Muller becomes Chancellor.

Sunday 28: Tomáš Masaryk, the 'father of Czechoslovakia' is elected President.

380 people are killed as a series of tornadoes hits the US midwest and south.

March/April 1920

Monday 29: Sir William Robertson, who enlisted as a private in the British Army in 1877, reaches the rank of Field Marshal, becoming the first man to rise from the lowest rank of the army to the highest.

Tuesday 30: Czechoslovakia flies its new flag (a blue triangle with red and white bands) for the first time.

Wednesday 31: The Church of Wales is disestablished, and becomes known as the Church 'in' rather than 'of' Wales.

Thursday 1: The German government approves the use of troops to put down the Ruhr uprising.

Friday 2 (Good Friday): Violence erupts in the Ruhr as government troops clash with communist irregulars.

Saturday 3: Novelist F Scott Fitzgerald (*The Great Gatsby*) marries Zelda Sayre at St Patrick's Cathedral, New York City.

Sunday 4 (Easter Day): Nine people are killed and 216 injured when violence erupts between arab and Jewish residents in Jerusalem, British Mandatory Palestine.

Armed communist volunteers in the Ruhr, Germany.

April 1920

Monday 5: English best-selling novelist Arthur Hailey (*Hotel, Airport, Wheels*) is born in Luton, Bedfordshire (died 2004).

Tuesday 6: The short lived (until 1922) Far Eastern Republic in eastern Siberia is declared independent of Soviet Russia.

Wednesday 7: Indian musican Sir Ravi Shankar is born in Varanasi, India (died 2012).

Ravi Shankar.

Thursday 8: Jazz singer Carmen McRae is born in Harlem, New York City (died 1994).

Friday 9: Lieutenant Norman Poole, Special Air Service, the first allied soldier to set foot in Normandy on D-Day, is born in Winchester, England (died 2015).

Engineer Alex Moulton CBE, inventor of hydroelastic suspension and the Moulton Mini folding bicycle, is born in England (died 2012).

Saturday 10: West Bromwich Albion wins the English Football League for the first time; England beats Scotland 5-4 at Hillsborough in the Home International Championship.

Sunday 11: Sultan Mehmed VI dissolves the Ottoman Parliament, as part of the winding down of the Ottoman Empire which finally ends in 1922.

Left: Sultan Mehmed VI.

April 1920

Monday 12: Chile's first saint, the Carmelite nun St Teresa of the Andes, dies aged 19.

Tuesday 13: Lieutenant Frederick Rothwell Holt is hanged at Strangeways Prison, Manchester, England, for the murder of twenty-six-year-old Kathleen Breaks.

John George Bartholomew.

Wednesday 14: Scottish mapmaker John George Bartholomew, known as the 'Prince of Cartography' and famous for naming the continent of Antarctica in 1890, dies aged 60.

Thursday 15: Two Italian born American anarchists, Nicola Sacco and Bartolomeo Vanzetti, kill two security guards while robbing a shoe factory in Braintree, Mass. After a series of lengthy trials the pair are eventually executed in 1927.

Friday 16: Swedish composer John Conrad Nordqvist dies aged 80.

Saturday 17: Salesman Joseph Yenowsky is arrested in Waterbury, Connecticut, and charged under the US 'red scare' laws for saying that Lenin is 'the most brainiest man on earth' in his workplace. He is later sentenced to six months' imprisonment.

Sunday 18: The IRA attacks a group of Royal Irish Constabulary officers leaving church in Kilmihil, County Clare. One officer is killed and several wounded.

April 1920

Monday 19: Representatives from the Allied nations meet in San Remo, Italy, to discuss the administration of mandated territories following the breakup of the Ottoman Empire.

Poster for the 1920 Olympics.

Tuesday 20: The winter section of the 1920 Olympics opens in Antwerp, Belgium (the first Winter Olympics is not held until 1924). The Olympic symbol of five interlocking rings is displayed for the first time.

Wednesday 21: Britain's future prime minister, Harold Macmillan marries Dorothy Cavendish, daughter of the 9th Duke of Devonshire, at St Margaret's Westminster.

Thursday 22: Hal March, host of TV quiz show *The $64,000 Question* is born in San Francisco, California (died 1970).

Friday 23: The Turkish parliament is founded by Mustafa Kemal Atatürk, in Ankara, following the closure of the Ottoman Parliament under Sultan Mehmed VI.

Saturday 24: Polish and anti-Soviet Ukrainian troops clash with the Red Army in the Ukraine.

Sunday 25: Magda Julin of Sweden beats team mate Svea Norén to win gold in the women's singles figure skating in the Olympics in Antwerp.

April/May 1920

Gillis Grafström

Monday 26: Canada beats Sweden 12-1 in the first ever Olympic ice hockey match.

Tuesday 27: Swedish Skater Gillis Grafström wins his first of three consecutive men's Olympic gold medals in Antwerp.

Wednesday 28: The Soviet Socialist Republic of Azerbaijan is established.

Thursday 29: English children's author and broadcaster Edward Blishen (*The God Beneath The Sea*) is born in Barnet, Hertfordshire (died 1996).

Friday 30: Wartime military conscription ends in Britain.

Saturday 1: Baseball legend Babe Ruth of the New York Yankees hits his 50th home run in a 6-0 win over the Boston Red Sox.

Sunday 2: The first game of the newly formed Negro National Baseball League takes place in Indianapolis, Indiana.

Left: Babe Ruth of the New York Yankees.

May 1920

Monday 3: An attempted Bolshevik coup ends in failure in the newly formed Democratic Republic of Georgia.

Tuesday 4: Margaret 'Margo' Durrell, sister of naturalist Gerald Durrell and writer Laurence Durrell is born in India (died 2007).

Wednesday 5: Britain's *Guardian* newspaper describes Russian composer Igor Stravinsky's new avant-garde piece, *Ragtime,* as 'utterly, hopelessly bad'.

Thursday 6: The British parliament discusses the possibility of producing a petrol substitute, known as 'power alcohol' in the UK rather than having to import fuel. The idea does not catch on..

Friday 7: Polish troops occupy Kiev in the Ukraine.

Saturday 8: IRA gunmen led by Mick Leahy capture Cloyne Barracks in County Cork.

Sunday 9: Novelist Richard Adams, author of *Watership Down*, is born in Newbury, Berkshire, England (died 2016).

Polish troops enter Kiev.

May 1920

Monday 10: British guitarist Bert Weedon OBE, inventor of the 'play in a day' learning system used by many guitarists including Paul McCartney and Eric Clapton, is born in London (died 2012).

Tuesday 11: IRA volunteers destroy the Royal Irish Constabulary barracks at Hollyford, County Tipperary.

Wednesday 12: An auction is announced in New York of the throne and other furniture belonging to the deposed Kaiser Wilhelm II of Germany.

Thursday 13: The body of a woman identified only as 'Countess W' is found in Lake Geneva, Switzerland. Clad in expensive furs and jewels the corpse bears a note stating 'I am a victim of the Bolsheviks'. She is thought to be the sixth exiled Russian to commit suicide in Geneva since the Russian revolution.

Lt Maria Bochkareva, the first Russian female army officer.

Friday 14: A delegation of Armenians in Paris begs the US government to intervene in the growing crisis in their country due to threats from Turkey on one side and the Soviet state of Azerbaijan on the other.

Saturday 15: Allied governments agree that war reparations of $750,000,000 per year for 30 years must be paid by Germany.

Sunday 16: Lt Maria Bochkareva, the first combatant woman officer in the White Russian army, is executed by the Bolsheviks.

May 1920

Monday 17: The first flight by Dutch airline KLM from Amsterdam to London takes place.

Tuesday 18: Karol Józef Wojtyła, later Pope John Paul II, is born in Wadowice, Poland (died 2005).

Wednesday 19: In the Mexican Revolution, the revolutionary troops of Álvaro Obregón enter Mexico City.

Thursday 20: Actress and singer Betty Driver MBE (Betty Williams in *Coronation Street*) is born in Leicester, England (died 2011).

Pope John Paul II.

Friday 21: Mexico's revolutionary leader Venustiano Carranza de la Garza is assassinated.

Saturday 22: Astrophysicist Thomas Gold, one of the first exponents of the 'steady state' theory of the universe, is born in Vienna, Austria (died 2004).

President Deschanel.

Sunday 23: An injured and delirious man clad only in pyjamas is found wandering along a railway line near Montargis, France; when questioned by a track worker he claims to be the President of France.

The man's story is found to be true; President Deschanel had fallen from the window of a sleeper train while under the influence of medication. He retires on medical grounds a few months later.

May 1920

David Lloyd George.

Monday 24: The greatest church union in the history of the USA takes place as the Northern and Southern Presbyterian Churches combine. The union includes the Dutch, German and Scots Presbyterian churches, forming a denomination of some two million adherents.

Tuesday 25: Britain's Prime Minister David Lloyd George summons representatives of the British Dominions to London for discussions on war reparations.

Wednesday 26: A failed anti-soviet uprising takes place in Ganja, Azerbaijan's second city.

Thursday 27: The government of the north western Russian province of Karelia introduces conscription for all men between 19 and 50 in an attempt to drive out invading Bolshevik forces.

Friday 28: Two police officers are killed when the IRA attacks Kilmallock Barracks in County Limerick.

Saturday 29: A 'radium rush' begins in Canada as deposits of the valuable mineral are found near the town of Kearney, Ontario.

23 people are killed when floods hit the town of Louth in Lincolnshire, England.

Sunday 30: Central New York is gridlocked after a steam pipe explodes on Fifth Avenue, shooting scalding water to a height of 200 feet; 65 homes are destroyed when a forest fire hits the town of St John, New Brunswick, Canada.

May/June 1920

Monday 31: 1200 Turkish troops are killed as the French army attempts to impose its League of Nations mandate in Syria.

Tuesday 1: Bolshevik forces are pushed back in the Ukraine, preventing them from advancing on Minsk.

Wednesday 2: US author Eugene O'Neill is awarded the Pulitzer Prize for his play, *Beyond the Horizon*.

Thursday 3: 2000 British marines are ordered to guard the coast of Ireland after the IRA wreck several coast guard stations and lighthouses, thought to be in preparation for the delivery of arms shipments.

Friday 4: The Treaty of Trianon is signed, formally ending the state of war between Hungary and the Allied powers, and ceding two-thirds of Hungary's territory to its neighbouring countries.

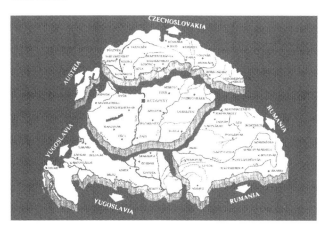

Map showing the break-up of Hungary by the Treaty of Trianon.

Saturday 5: Bolshevik troops rally in the Ukraine, and begin advancing towards Kiev.

Sunday 6: The Vlora War, which formally began on 4 June, intensifies as Italian troops invade Albania to enforce their League of Nations mandate.

June 1920

A howitzer is moved into the new Imperial War Museum, London.

Monday 7: A final legal challenge to revoke Prohibition fails in the US supreme court.

Tuesday 8: Cincinatti Reds baseball player Edd Roush becomes the only player in major league history to be sent off by an umpire for falling asleep during a game.

Wednesday 9: HM King George V opens London's Imperial War Museum at Crystal Palace.

Thursday 10: Following the opening of the judiciary to women in 1919, it is announced that 45 women magistrates have been appointed in England and one in Wales.

Friday 11: The US Republican Party nominates Warren G Harding as their Presidential candidate.

British East Africa is renamed Kenya.

Saturday 12: The Red Army seizes Kiev in the Ukraine.

Sunday 13: Essad Pasha, former Prime Minister of Albania, is assassinated in France while representing his country at the Paris Peace Conference.

Essad Pasha.

June 1920

Monday 14: German philosopher Max Weber, one of the founders of sociology, dies aged 56.

Tuesday 15: A black circus worker is lynched after a 5000-strong mob breaks into a jail in Duluth, Minnesotta, and holds a kangaroo-court trial of six suspects held following an attack on a local girl.

Wednesday 16: After warnings from the League of Nations about a possible Bolshevik attack on Persia, Russia announces it has no plans to take over the country.

Beryl Reid: born 17 June 1920.

Thursday 17: Actress Beryl Reid OBE (*The Belles of St Trinians, The Killing of Sister George*) is born in Hereford, England (died 1996).

Friday 18: Five people are killed in sectarian clashes in Londonderry, Ireland.

Actor Ian Carmichael OBE (*I'm Alright Jack, School for Scoundrels, The World of Wooster*) is born in Kingston upon Hull, England.

Saturday 19: The future Pope John Paul II is baptised in Wadowice, Poland.

Sunday 20: Two people are killed and a policeman injured in clashes between black radicals and whites in Chicago, Illinois following a flag-burning incident.

June 1920

Monday 21: Londonderry is put under martial law; shops and businesses are closed due to the ongoing street fighting.

Tuesday 22: Greek troops seize territory in Anatolia held by the Turkish nationalists.

Greek troops engage in Turkey.

Wednesday 23: Prime Minister David Lloyd George denies that Britain is monopolising middle eastern oilfields under the British Mandate in Mesopotamia.

Thursday 24: One person is killed as huge floods hit New York City after 3/4 of an inch of rain falls in five minutes.

Friday 25: Mahatma Gandhi threatens to advise Indians to withdraw all support for the British government in India if it continues its policy of military action against Islamic Turkey.

Saturday 26: Rioting and industrial action spreads across Germany in response to food shortages.

Sunday 27: Three senior British army officers are attacked and wounded by IRA gunmen near Cork, Ireland. One of the men, General Cuthbert Lucas, is kidnapped but escapes on 31 July.

June/July 1920

Monday 28: The Roman Catholic church in France allows deaf-mute priests to celebrate mass for the first time.

Tuesday 29: Hollywood special effects expert and model-make Ray Harryhausen (*Clash of the Titans*) is born in Los Angeles, California (died 2013).

Wednesday 30: Greek troops seize the city of Balikesir in Marmara, Turkey.

Wimbledon champion Suzanne Lenglen.

Thursday 1: At the Wimbledon tennis finals, France's Suzanne Lenglen is the women's champion and two days later, Bill Tilden becomes the first American to win the mens' title.

Friday 2: *The New York Sun* reports that following prohibition, a pint of whisky is now selling for $10 on the black market, or roughly one third to one quarter of a working man's weekly wage.

Saturday 3: Britain's first rollercoaster, the Scenic Railway, opens at the Dreamland amusement park in Margate, Kent.

Sunday 4: At the war reparations conference in Spa, Belgium, German representatives announce that they cannot afford to pay the punitive damages demanded by the Versailles treaty.

July 1920

Monday 5: Airmail services begin between London and Amsterdam.

Tuesday 6: President Deschanel of France purchases an aeroplane for state visits. Satirists seize on the news following Deschanel's accidental fall from his sleeper train in May.

Wednesday 7: Arthur Meighen becomes Prime Minister of Canada.

Thursday 8: Godtfred Kirk Christiansen, inventor of Lego, is born in Billund, Denmark (died 1995).

Friday 9: Britain's Prime Minister David Lloyd George rejects a plea from Poland for aid in fighting the Soviets.

Saturday 10: The champion racehorse Man o' War sets a new speed record of a mile and a furlong (1.125 miles/1.81 km) in 1 minute 49 seconds, ridden by John P Grier at the Aqueduct Race Track, New York City.

Sunday 11: The states of East and West Prussia vote to become part of Germany, with a 'Polish corridor' running through them to the Baltic Sea.

Champion racehorse Man o'War.

July 1920

Monday 12: Lithuania becomes independent of soviet Russia.

Tuesday 13: Boxing promoter Tex Rickard announces plans to develop New York's Madison Square Garden into a major venue seating 20,000.

Wednesday 14: The Allied powers at the Spa conference in Belgium threaten Germany with occupation if it fails to pay reparations.

Allied officers gather in Spa, Belgium.

Thursday 15: The Allies force Germany to pay the cost of its occupying troops.

Friday 16: The 1919 Treaty of Saint-Germain-en-Laye comes into effect. It formally ends the war between Germany and Austria and the Allies and ends the Austro-Hungarian Empire.

Saturday 17: US physicist Gordon Gould, inventor of the laser beam, is born in New York City (died 2005).

Sunday 18: War hero Prince Joachim of Hohenzollern, youngest son of Germany's Kaiser, commits suicide aged 29.

July 1920

Andrew Bonar Law.

Monday 19: The Second Congress of the Communist International begins in St Petersburg and Moscow.

Tuesday 20: Britain's Leader of the House of Commons, Andrew Bonar Law, announces that despite large numbers of troops being sent to restore order in Ireland, martial law will not be declared in the province.

Wednesday 21: Britain's Prime Minister David Lloyd George heads the Interallied Mission to Poland, to influence Polish foreign policy against the Soviets.

Thursday 22: Poland offers a peace treaty to the Soviets, which is refused.

Friday 23: Frank Courtney wins the Aerial Derby air race around London, completing a circuit starting from Hendon with an average speed of 153.5mph.

Saturday 24: The French army defeats Syria at the Battle of Maysalun, occupying Damascus and deposing King Faisal I.

Sunday 25: Seven bathers drown during freak tidal conditions off the coast at Coney Island, NY.

King Faisal I of Syria.

July/August 1920

Monday 26: Most of southern Slovakia is put under martial law following attempts by foreign Bolshevik agitators to disrupt the harvest.

Tuesday 27: Belgian cyclist Philippe Thys wins the Tour de France in 231 hours 7m 15 seconds. Monsieur Thys is the first cyclist to win the Tour three times.

The US yacht *Resolute* wins the Americas Cup race, beating *Shamrock IV* of the Royal Ulster Yacht Club.

Wednesday 28: After living as a fugitive for years, Mexican revolutionary Pancho Villa comes out of hiding and surrenders to President Adolfo de la Huerta.

The UK's first women jurors begin service in Bristol, England.

Americas Cup winner *Resolute*.

Thursday 29: Irish republican leader Eamonn de Valera announces he will accept British Dominion status for Ireland rather than fight on for full independence.

Friday 30: The first World Scout Jamboree is held in London.

Saturday 31: The Communist Party of Great Britain is founded in London.

Sunday 1: The British government announces that IRA and Sinn Fein insurgents will be tried under martial rather than civil law.

August 1920

Monday 2: British PM David Lloyd George announces in Parliament that no negotiations over Irish independence will be entertained until order is restored in the province.

Tuesday 3: Detective writer PD James OBE (Baroness James of Holland Park) author of the Cordelia Gray and Adam Dalgleish mysteries, is born in Oxford, England (died 2014).

Wednesday 4: The provisional Irish Republican parliament bans emigration from Ireland. The ban has no legal standing but it is thought it will be influential.

Thursday 5: Two men are killed and 35 injured, including the chief of police, as striking tram workers clash with police in Denver, Colorado.

Friday 6: Following a breakdown in peace talks, Soviet forces continue their advance on Warsaw, Poland.

Saturday 7: Large numbers of residents, including US aid workers, evacuate from Warsaw.

Sunday 8: In the face of the Soviet advance, the Polish government evacuates Warsaw and moves to Krakow.

Polish troops on the outskirts of Warsaw await the Reds.

August 1920

Forward, Warsaw! by Zdzisław Jasiński, depicting Poland's miraculous victory.

Monday 9: Child star Allen Hoskins ('Farina' in Our Gang) is born in Boston, MA (died 1980).

Tuesday 10: Representatives of the Allied forces and Sultan Mehmet VI sign the Treaty of Sèvres in France, beginning the breakup of the seven-hundred-year-old Ottoman Empire.

Wednesday 11: The Soviet-Latvian Peace Treaty is signed, recognising Latvia as an independent country.

Thursday 12: The Battle of Warsaw begins.

Friday 13: Ted Ray of Britain's Channel Islands wins the US Open golf tournament at the Inverness Club, Ohio.

Saturday 14: The summer section of the 1920 Olympics opens in Antwerp, Belgium.

Sunday 15: The tide turns in favour of the Poles, as Sikorsky's Fifth Army forces the Soviets to begin retreating from Warsaw. The decisive event is known as the 'Miracle on the Vistula' as it prevents the fall of Poland to Bolshevism.

August 1920

Monday 16: British premier David Lloyd George breaks off negotiations with trade union representatives after they threaten a general strike if Britain sends military aid to Poland against the Bolsheviks.

Tuesday 17: Ray Chapman, 29, of the Cleveland Indians dies after being hit on the head by a ball in a match against the Yankees the previous day. He remains the only major league baseball player to die from injuries sustained in a game.

Memorial to Ray Chapman at Progressive Field, Cleveland, Ohio. Chapman remains the only major league baseball player to be fatally injured during a game.

Wednesday 18: Academy-Award-winning Actress Shelly Winters (*The Diary of Anne Frank, A Patch of Blue*) is born in St Louis, Missouri (died 2006).

Thursday 19: The Second Silesian Uprising begins as ethnic Poles in Germany's Silesia region fight for independence.

Friday 20: The USA's first commercial radio station, the Detroit News Radiophone (8MK), begins broadcasting. It remains in operation under the name WWJ-AM.

Saturday 21: Christopher Robin Milne, son of AA Milne and inspiration for the character of Christopher Robin in the *Winnie the Pooh* books, is born in London (died 1996).

Sunday 22: The Country Party, now the National Party of Australia, is formed under Nelson Pollard.

August 1920

Monday 23: US swimmer Warren Kealoha wins the first of his two Olympic gold medals at Antwerp for the 100m backstroke.

Tuesday 24: The Red Army is reported to be in full retreat in Poland, with 50,000 prisoners taken by the Poles.

Wednesday 25: US swimmer Ethelda Bleibtrey wins gold at the Olympics in Antwerp. She is the first American woman to win an Olympic swimming title.

Thursday 26: The Nineteenth Amendment to the US Constitution is passed, guaranteeing women the right to vote.

Friday 27: Irish-Americans in New York City demonstrate against British rule in Ireland, persuading longshoremen to refuse to unload eight British liners. It is said to be the first purely political strike in US history.

Saturday 28: The Bukhara Operation begins; Soviet troops attack the Emirate of Bukhara in what is now Uzbekistan.

Sunday 29: US swimmer Ethelda Bleibtrey wins her third gold medal at the Olympics in Antwerp, with fellow American swimmers Aileen Riggin and Duke Kahanamoku also winning gold.

US swimming champions: Ethelda Bleitrey and Warren Kealoha.

August/September 1920

Monday 30: New York City is gridlocked by a subway strike; the chaos is increased as commuters refuse to obey police orders to drive one way only over the Brooklyn Bridge.

Tuesday 31: Two people are killed and sixteen injured when an elevator plummets ten stories to the ground in the Clarendon Building on New York's Eighteenth Street.

Wednesday 1: The state of Greater Lebanon is established as a French colony to be ruled under the League of Nations mandate.

The US Navy submarine *S5* sinks 181 feet to the sea bed during trials off the Delaware Capes, and is presumed lost.

Thursday 2: Four pedestrians are killed in traffic accidents in New York City as the transport strike continues to cause chaos on the roads.

Friday 3: Following severe rioting in Belfast, Ireland, two warships and large numbers of British troops are rushed to the province to protect the shipyards from IRA attacks.

Saturday 4: The US Navy submarine *S5*, which sank on 1 September manages to partly re-surface; almost asphyxiated, the crew are rescued when a passing steamship spots the tip of the vessel's turret.

Sunday 5: Hollywood actor Robert Harron, 27, who appeared in *Birth of a Nation*, dies from injuries sustained after accidentally shooting himself while unpacking a pistol on 1 September.

Robert Harron.

September 1920

Monday 6: A trial run is held for a coast-to-coast US airmail service, cutting delivery time from 100 hours by train to 60.5 hours.

Tuesday 7: British PM David Lloyd George announces that he will release the Mayor of Cork, Terence MacSwiney, imprisoned on sedition charges, if IRA violence ceases; the request is rejected.

Wednesday 8: The city-state of Fiume, formerly of Italy but ceded by the Allies to Croatia, declares itself to be independent under the rule of the soldier-poet General Gabriele d'Annunzio. Fiume is defeated and absorbed into Italy by the end of 1920.

Thursday 9: British actor Michael Aldridge (Seymour in *Last of the Summer Wine*) is born in Glastonbury (died 1994).

Friday 10: Four people are killed when avalanches hit the Swiss and Italian alps following a severe earthquake.

Saturday 11: The first all-woman jury in the USA is sworn in to decide an assault case in Chicago, Illinois.

Sunday 12: The Patriarchy of the Serbian Orthodox Church is re-established, 156 years after its abolition by the Ottomans.

The 1920 Olympics closes in Antwerp, Belgium.

Left: General Gabriele d'Annunzio, ruler of the short-lived independent state of Fiume.

September 1920

Monday 13: The London *Times* reveals that Bolsheviks have attempted to give a £75,000 bribe to the trade union *Herald* newspaper.

Tuesday 14: Plans are announced for improving Plymouth Rock, Boston, where the first Mayflower pilgrims arrived in 1620.

Wednesday 15: Jan Černý becomes Prime Minister of Czechoslovakia.

Thursday 16: 38 people are killed and 143 injured when a bomb explodes on Wall Street, New York City. The perpetrators are never identified but are thought to be Italian anarchists.

Friday 17: The USA's National Football League is founded.

Saturday 18: Tennis star Edwin Fischer is arrested after claims that he warned of the bomb attack of 16 September. He claims he is psychic and is eventually committed to an asylum.

Sunday 19: The Saunders-Kittiwake experimental flying boat makes its first test flight from the Isle of Wight, England.

Bomb damage on Wall Street.

September 1920

Monday 20: Three British soldiers are fatally wounded during an ambush in Dublin; gunman Kevin Barry, 18, is arrested and in November becomes the first Irish nationalist to be executed since the Easter Uprising of 1916.

Tuesday 21: The Netherlands announces a build up of its armed forces due to the 'uncertain situation' in Europe.

Kevin Barry.

Wednesday 22: London's Metropolitan Police forms the legendary motorised Flying Squad (also known as the 'Sweeney'), to combat armed robbery.

Six Royal Irish Constabulary officers are killed in an IRA ambush in Rineen, County Clare.

Thursday 23: Actor Mickey Rooney of the Andy Hardy film series is born in New York City (died 2014).

Friday 24: Russian jewellery designer Peter Carl Fabergé, inventor of the Fabergé Egg, dies aged 74.

Saturday 25: US prohibition enforcement agents pour 21,000 bottles of confiscated beer into the Chicago River.

Sunday 26: Officers of the British auxiliary police (the 'Black and Tans') burn down several houses in Kilkee, County Clare, in reprisals for IRA attacks.

Right: Mickey Rooney.

September/October 1920

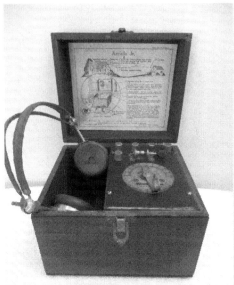

The first Westinghouse radio set.

Monday 27: Russian Bolshevik forces sue for peace with Poland.

Tuesday 28: Baseball player Eddie Cicotte confesses to a grand jury that he and several others conspired to fix the 1919 World Series.

Wednesday 29: The first commercial radio sets go on sale in the USA, manufactured by Westinghouse and retailing for $10.

Thursday 30: A police inspector is killed in an IRA ambush near Tobercurry, County Sligo.

Friday 1: Actor Walter Matthau (*The Odd Couple*) is born in New York City (died 2000).

Walter Matthau: born 1 October.

Saturday 2: King Alexander of Greece is attacked by a pet monkey in the grounds of his palace in Tatoi; he dies of his injuries on 25 October.

Sunday 3: The Prix de l'Arc de Triomph horse race is first run at Longchamps, Paris.

October 1920

Monday 4: British war hero Colonel Sir Ronald 'Tommy' MacPherson, CBE MC and two bars, known as the 'kilted killer', is born in Edinburgh, Scotland (died 2014).

Tuesday 5: Following the defeat of Red Army forces, the Polish-Lithuanian border is fixed, separating Lithuania from Russia.

The British government announces a system of hand signals for road traffic which is eventually published as the Highway Code in 1931.

Wednesday 6: Two brothers oppose each other in baseball's World Series for the first time: 'Doc' Johnston for the Cleveland Indians and sibling Jimmy Johnston for the Brooklyn Robins.

Thursday 7: The first women are admitted as full members of Oxford University. Women had been permitted to study in Oxford since the 1870s but were not awarded degrees.

Friday 8: US author Frank Herbert, whose book *Dune* becomes the best selling science fiction book of all time, is born in Tacoma, Washington (died 1984).

Saturday 9: Polish troops invade Lithuania and seize the capital, Vilnius.

Sunday 10: Residents of central Europe's Carinthia region vote to become part of Austria rather than Yugoslavia.

Poster urging young Carinthians to join Austria or face military conscription.

October 1920

Monday 11: Two British army officers and a civilian are fatally wounded during a shootout with the IRA in Drumcondra, Dublin.

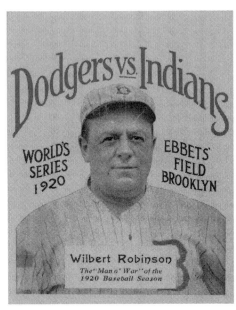

Programme for the World Series final.

Tuesday 12: The Cleveland Indians win the 1920 Baseball World Series.

Wednesday 13: Large ecstatic crowds gather in Cleveland, Ohio to celebrate the Cleveland Indians' victory over the Brooklyn Robins in the final of the baseball World Series the previous day.

Thursday 14: A peace treaty is signed between the Finnish and Soviet governments in Tartu, Finland.

Montgomery Clift.

Friday 15: Author Mario Puzo (*The Godfather*) is born in Hell's Kitchen, New York City (died 1999).

Saturday 16: Polish troops capture several Soviet cities including Minsk in Belarus, after which a ceasefire comes into effect.

Sunday 17: Actor Montgomery Clift (*From Here to Eternity, The Misfits*) is born in Omaha, Nebraska (died 1966).

October 1920

The last Grand Vizier.

Monday 18: Ahmed Tevfik Pasha is appointed as the last Grand Vizier (prime minister) of the Ottoman Empire.

Tuesday 19: The Estonian-Latvian border is agreed in Riga under British arbitration.

Wednesday 20: Women's suffrage campaigner Sylvia Pankhurst is sentenced to six months' imprisonment for writing seditious newspaper articles.

Transsexual murderer Eugenia Falleni, whose strange case shocked Australia.

Thursday 21: The conviction of the transsexual woman Eugenia Falleni for the murder of her 'wife', Annie Birkett, causes a sensation in Australia. Falleni, who had lived as a man for many years, is sentenced to life imprisonment.

Friday 22: American psychologist Timothy Leary, who promoted LSD and coined the phrase 'turn on, tune in, drop out', is born in Springfield, MA (died 1996).

Saturday 23: 23 demonstrators are shot dead by police in Port Elizabeth, South Africa, during protests over the arrest of a trade union leader.

Sunday 24: Crooner Steve Conway (known as 'England's Bing Crosby) is born in London (died 1952).

October 1920

Monday 25: The Mayor of Cork, Terence McSwiney, dies in Brixton prison after a 78 day hunger strike in protest against British rule in Ireland.

Terence McSwiney.

Tuesday 26: Álvaro Obregón becomes President of Mexico.

Wednesday 27: Police intercept a letter written by imprisoned radical Sylvia Pankhurst to Lenin, asking for help in her efforts towards a communist uprising.

Thursday 28: The Treaty of Paris is signed, ceding the region of Bessarabia (now Moldova) to Romania; it never comes into force as Japan refuses to ratify the deal, due to a secret deal with the Soviets.

Friday 29: 19 men drown when the US steamer *Cape Fear* sinks in Narragansett Bay near Newport, Rhode Island.

Saturday 30: Violence worsens across Ireland, with 11 dead in clashes between the police/army and IRA.

Sunday 31: Large crowds gather in Cork, Ireland, for the funeral of Mayor Terence MacSwiney who died after a 78-day hunger strike in protest against British rule.

Left: Sylvia Pankhurst.

November 1920

Charles Ponzi.

Monday 1: Italian-American swindler Charles Ponzi is sentenced to five years in prison for his multi-million dollar stock-market scam known as the 'Ponzi Scheme'.

Tuesday 2: Republican senator Warren G Harding defeats Democrat James M Cox to become the 29th President of the USA. The country's second radio station, KDKA in Pittsburgh begins broadcasting with news of the victory.

Wednesday 3: The 'Battle of Ballinalee' takes place as the IRA clashes with the police and army in Ballinale, County Longford.

Thursday 4: Fierce debates take place in Britain's House of Commons over the worsening situation in Ireland, with nationalist MPs calling for an independent enquiry into the deaths of civilians.

Friday 5: British cycling champion Tommy Godwin is born in Connecticut, USA (died 2012).

Saturday 6: Soviet troops enter the Crimea and clash with White Russian forces.

Sunday 7: The city of Boston, Massachussetts, announces it will admit women to its police force.

Warren G Harding, 29th President of the United States (1920-1923).

November 1920

Monday 8: Cartoon character Rupert the Bear makes his first appearance in print, in a *Daily Express* strip.

Tuesday 9: DH Lawrence's controversial novel *Women in Love* is published in the USA.

Wednesday 10: The body of the Unknown Warrior, an unidentified soldier of the Great War 'known only to God', is brought from France to London in an oak coffin made from trees from the Hampton Court estate.

London's Cenotaph is unveiled.

Thursday 11: A guard of honour of 100 Victoria Cross holders led by HM King George V escorts the body of the Unknown Warrior through vast silent crowds in London. The cortege stops for the unveiling of the new Cenotaph war memorial in Whitehall; the body is then buried in the nave of Westminster Abbey.

Friday 12: The Treaty of Rapello is signed, agreeing the border between Italy and Yugoslavia.

Saturday 13: The last 150,000 survivors of the White Russian (Czarist) forces and civilian refugees are evacuated from the Crimea on board 126 ships; most of those left behind are killed by advancing Bolshevik forces.

Sunday 14: The Bolshevik army occupies Sevastopol, capital of the Crimea.

November 1920

Monday 15: The first full performance of *The Planets* suite by Gustav Holst is given in London by the London Symphony Orchestra.

Tuesday 16: The Australian airline Qantas (Queensland and Northern Territory Aviation Service) is founded.

Wednesday 17: The League of Nations ratifies the constitution of the new Free City of Danzig in the Polish Corridor.

Thursday 18: British chess expert John Herbert White, co-author of *Modern Chess Openings*, dies aged 40.

Friday 19: Hollywood star Gene Tierney (*Laura, Heaven Can Wait*) is born in New York City (died 1991).

Saturday 20: Prince Arthur of Connaught becomes Governor General of South Africa.

Sunday 21: 'Bloody Sunday': 14 British agents are shot dead by the IRA in Dublin; British soldiers, claiming to have been fired on, kill 14 spectators at a football match at Croke Park.

Top: Gustav Holst. Middle: Gene Tierney. Bottom: Prince Arthur of Connaught.

November 1920

Above: poster for *The Mark of Zorro* released on 27 November.

Monday 22: British actress Anne Crawford (*Millions Like Us*) is born in Haifa, Palestine (died 1956).

Tuesday 23: Royal Irish Constabulary officer Michael Dennehy is kidnapped by the IRA in Strokestown, County Roscommon, presumed murdered.

Wednesday 24: Two people are killed and 15 injured when a bomb is thrown into a crowd in Cork, Ireland; Dublin jails are reported to be 'full to overflowing' following mass arrests of IRA suspects.

Thursday 25: Racing driver Gaston Chevrolet, 28, brother of Chevrolet Motors founder Louis, is killed during a motor race at Beverley Hills Speedway, California.

Friday 26: The Irish politician and founder of the Sinn Fein party, Arthur Griffith, is arrested in Dublin on charges of sedition.

Saturday 27: *The Mark of Zorro*, starring Douglas Fairbanks, is released in US cinemas.

Sunday 28: 17 British police auxiliaries are killed by the IRA in an ambush at Kilmichael, County Cork.

November/December 1920

Monday 29: The last wartime rationing ends in Britain as sugar becomes freely available.

Tuesday 30: Hollywood star Virginia Mayo (*The Best Years of Our Lives*) is born in St Louis, Missouri (died 2005).

Wednesday 1: After a ten year armed struggle the Mexican Revolution ends as Revolutionary General Alvaro Obregón becomes President.

Virginia Mayo.

Thursday 2: Five people, including English ballet star Eva Luscomb, die in an apartment building blaze on West 57th Street, New York City.

Friday 3: The Treaty of Alexandrapol ends the Turkish-Armenian War.

Saturday 4: British comedy actor Michael Bates (Cyril in *Last of the Summer Wine* and Ranji Ram in *It Ain't Half Hot Mum*) is born in Jhansi, India (died 1978).

Sunday 5: Greeks vote in a referendum to restore their monarchy under King Constantine I.

Right: HM King Constantine I of Greece.

December 1920

Monday 6: Jazz pianist Dave Brubeck, famous for *Take Five*, is born in Concord, California (died 2012).

Tuesday 7: Outgoing US President Woodrow Wilson gives his eighth State of the Union Address.

Wednesday 8: Heavyweight boxer Mickey Shannon is killed by a knock-out blow during a bout with Al Roberts in Jersey City, New Jersey.

Thursday 9: British PM David Lloyd George meets for talks with Australian Archbishop Joseph Clune, intermediary for the Irish nationalists.

Friday 10: Martial law is declared in the Irish counties of Cork, Kerry, Limerick and Tipperary.

Saturday 11: Serious damage by fire is caused in Cork, Ireland, as British forces undertake reprisals for the killing of an auxiliary policeman in the city.

Sunday 12: Maurice Ravel's ballet *La Valse* premieres in Paris.

Burnt-out buildings in Cork, Ireland.

December 1920

Monday 13: The Haribo confectionary company, inventor of the 'gummi bear', is founded in Bonn, Germany. The name is an acronym formed from **Ha**ns **Ri**egel, **Bo**nn.

Tuesday 14: Jack Dempsey knocks out Bill Brennan to win the World Heavyweight boxing title in New York City.

Wednesday 15: Four people are killed in Britain's first fatal commercial air accident, as a Handley Page aircraft crashes in the north London suburb of Golders Green shortly after takeoff from Hendon Aerodrome.

Jack Dempsey, heavyweight champion.

Thursday 16: At least 100,000 people perish when a massive earthquake and a series of aftershocks hit the Haiyuan region of China.

Friday 17: The colony of German South West Africa comes under South African control following the break up of Germany's African Empire in the Treaty of Versailles.

Saturday 18: British naval hero and scuba-diving pioneer Lt Cdr Ian Edward Fraser VC, DSC, is born in London (died 2008).

Sunday 19: HM King Constantine I is restored to the Greek throne.

December 1920

Enrico Caruso.

Monday 20: British-born comedian Bob Hope becomes a US citizen.

Tuesday 21: The Ziegield Follies musical *Sally*, written by Jerome Kern, opens on Broadway.

Wednesday 22: The Soviets publish their first Five Year Plan for economic development.

Thursday 23: Britain passes the Government of Ireland Act to partition the province into semi-autonomous Northern and Southern states.

Friday 24: The great opera singer Enrico Caruso gives his final public performance, in *La Juive* in New York City.

Dick, Kerr's Ladies football team.

December 1920

Saturday 25 (Christmas Day): The biggest home win of the 1920-21 English football season takes place, as Burnley defeat Sheffield United 6-0.

Sunday 26: The largest attendance on record for a Womens' Football Association match is recorded when 53,000 watch Dick, Kerr's Ladies (later Preston Ladies) v St Helen's Ladies in Liverpool.

Monday 27: Ray Parer, the first pilot to attempt a circumnavigation of Australia, wins the Victorian Aerial Derby in an Airco DH4 biplane.

Jack Lord.

Tuesday 28: Princess Antoinette of Monaco (sister of Prince Rainier) is born in Paris (died 2011).

Winston Churchill.

Wednesday 29: Winston Churchill grants the London *Times* permission to publish his memoirs, for a fee of £5000.

Thursday 30: US actor Jack Lord (Steve McGarrett in *Hawaii Five-O*) is born in New York City (died 1998).

Friday 31: Country singer Rex Allen (the 'Arizona Cowboy') is born near Willcox, Arizona (died 1999).

The Treaty of Tartu is ratified, establishing the border between Estonia and Russia.

Birthday Notebooks

Handy 60 page ruled notebooks with a significant event from the year heading each page.

Available from Montpelier Publishing at Amazon.

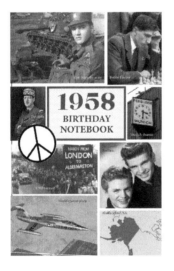

Made in United States
Orlando, FL
15 January 2022